RELIGIOUS STUDIES DEPT.

D1686032

THE WAY OF THE SIKH

THE WAY OF THE SIKH

by

W. H. McLEOD

illustrated by

DESMOND KNIGHT

HULTON EDUCATIONAL PUBLICATIONS

©
W. H. McLeod
1975

ISBN 0 7175 0731 9

First Published 1975
by
HULTON EDUCATIONAL PUBLICATIONS LTD
Raans Road, Amersham, Bucks.

Reprinted 1978
Reprinted 1982

Printed and bound in Great Britain
at The Pitman Press, Bath

ACKNOWLEDGEMENTS

The author acknowledges with gratitude comments and advice on the text received from Professor Harbans Singh and Shaun McLeod. He also thanks Miss E. I. Marshall for typing the text.

CONTENTS

8

CONTENTS

A Sikh

Who is a Sikh?

It is very easy to recognise a Sikh man. His wife and daughters may appear the same as other women from India, but the man himself has a special appearance. The two things which are most obvious are his turban and his beard. His turban sits low over his ears and then sweeps up each side of his forehead to form an upside-down V. Under the turban he will have long hair drawn upwards and tied in a neat knot on the top of his head, because baptised Sikhs are not allowed to cut their hair.

This refusal to cut their hair also explains their beards. A Sikh's beard may be long and bushy or it may be tightly rolled. If he is a devout Sikh it will never be touched by scissors or razor. One other thing you will notice worn by a devout Sikh is a steel bangle.

Although Sikh women do not wear turbans they observe the same rules concerning uncut hair and the steel bangle. They do so because these are two of the rules laid down for all Sikhs by the tenth and last of the great teachers of the Sikh religion. Sikhs are the followers of the ten Gurus. The word Guru means Master or Great Teacher, and Sikhs believe that religious truth is to be found in the teachings of their ten Masters. The first Guru was born in India more than

11

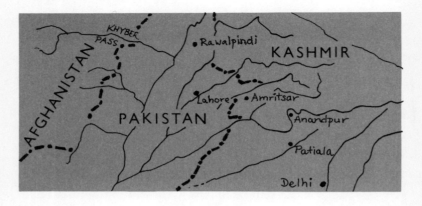

five hundred years ago. As each died he was succeeded by another until the tenth Guru died almost three hundred years ago.

Today Sikhs are to be seen in most countries of the world. Large numbers have come to England in recent years, although not all have retained their beards and turbans. Almost all the Sikh people in England have come direct from that part of India in which all the Gurus lived. This is the Punjab. To this day the vast majority of Sikhs still live in the Punjab and regard it as their homeland.

Sikhs have been famous as soldiers and many of them continue to serve in the Indian Army. Their religion began, however, in a very different way. The first Gurus stressed peace. It was only as enemies began to threaten them that the Sikhs turned to arms and became famous as warriors.

12

The Early Life of Guru Nanak

Nanak (nah-nuck), the first of the ten Gurus, was born in 1469. His father, Kalu, was a government official in a village forty miles from the great city of Lahore. It was in this village that Nanak was born and grew to manhood.

In later years his followers recorded stories of his childhood which pointed to his future greatness as a religious teacher. On one occasion the child Nanak was

Nanak sleeping

13

sent to graze the family cattle outside the village. Instead of watching the cattle he fell asleep and the cattle began to eat a neighbour's crop. The angry neighbour ran to the village headman to complain. Nanak, when summoned to explain his misconduct, replied that his cattle had done no harm. A messenger, sent to examine the crop, returned to report that Nanak spoke the truth. The ruined crop had been restored by a miracle.

On another occasion the village headman saw Nanak sleeping in the shadow of a tree. When he returned some hours later he found that, although the sun had moved round, the shadow of this particular tree had remained in the same place. During the whole day Nanak had been protected from the fierce rays of the sun.

These two stories were a way of showing later Sikhs that God's blessing was upon Nanak from his earliest childhood. Another popular story illustrated the kind of message which Nanak was to preach as a man. His father wanted him to become a trader. As soon as Nanak was old enough Kalu gave him a sum of money and sent him to the nearest market-town to see what bargains he could get. On the way Nanak encountered a group of starving men. When he reached the town he spent his father's money on food for the starving men and returned empty-handed. The story illustrates Nanak's concern for charity and kindness rather than for making money.

Guru Nanak's Travels

In the India of his time it was usual for parents to arrange the marriages of their children and to do so while they were still quite young. Nanak's parents arranged for him to be married to a girl called Sulakhani and later two sons were born to them.

His parents also found work for him in the town of Sultanpur where he was put in charge of the governor's grainstore. As he carried out his duties in Sultanpur there grew within him the belief that he had been called by God to a special mission. Everywhere people lived in ignorance and suffering. It was his duty to travel amongst them, teaching them the way of salvation.

While still a young man Nanak left his work in Sultanpur and began a long period of travels. For many years he journeyed on foot around India and other nearby countries, preaching to all who would listen to him. In doing so he spoke to people who were either Hindus or Muslims. He did not tell them to give up being Hindu or Muslim. Instead he tried to persuade them that it mattered little whether they were Hindu or Muslim, provided that they believed in the one God and lived a life of kindness to all men.

Many stories are told of this period in his life. One

Guru Nanak and companions

which shows the importance of honest labour is set in a small Punjab town called Eminabad. When he arrived in Eminabad Guru Nanak stayed at the house of a poor carpenter called Lalo. A rich man, hearing of Nanak's

16

arrival, invited him to a feast. When Nanak refused to come the rich man sent servants to bring him by force. He then demanded an explanation for Nanak's refusal. In reply Nanak took rich food from the feast in one hand and coarse food from Lalo's house in the other. When he squeezed both pieces of food blood dripped from the rich food and milk from the coarse. The story is intended to show that they who earn their bread by honest labour are pure, whereas others who gain riches by harshness and cruelty are evil. The lowly carpenter Lalo was pure. The rich man who had made his money by mistreating others was evil and impure.

Another popular story serves to illustrate the most important feature of Nanak's teaching. During his travels Nanak was accompanied by a disciple called Mardana. On one occasion, while passing through dense jungle, they were seized by a fearsome monster who prepared to eat them. Mardana was put in a cauldron of oil and set over a fire. At Nanak's command Mardana repeated the name of God and the oil, instead of coming to the boil, grew cooler. Once again the story is intended to teach a particular lesson. The lesson to be taken from this one is that they who repeat the name of God will be preserved from all evils because in the end they will obtain salvation.

The Message of Guru Nanak

The story of the monster's cauldron raises the question of what it means to "repeat the Name of God". It is a very important question because it brings us to the heart of Nanak's teaching. When Nanak had completed his travels he returned to the Punjab and settled down

Ik-onkar: symbol of God

with his family in the village of Kartarpur. There he continued to compose the hymns which tell us what he meant by "repeating the Name of God" or (to use another of his expressions) "remembering the Name of God".

Guru Nanak's teachings begin with a belief in one God. How can man know God? Nanak says that man

18

can know God simply by looking at the world around him. All that we see tells us something about God because it is all a part of God. We know that God is strong and mighty because only a strong and mighty God could create the world. We also know that he is a God of grace who cares. One of the reasons we know he cares is that he provides the means of knowing him and of finding salvation.

God is pure and good. Man, on the other hand, is wayward, impure, and prone to do wrong. Because of his evil thoughts and deeds he is doomed to be born

Guru Nanak teaching

19

again and again. Only when he attains to purity and true goodness can he break the chain of rebirths and obtain that perfect peace which for Nanak is salvation.

How can he do this? First, he must learn to recognise the "Name" of God. By this Nanak means all that can be known about God. Because all that we see around us is a part of God it is also a part of the Name of God. Next he must "remember the Name of God", which means that he must spend a part of each day thinking about God. This is called meditation. It can be done silently, or by saying over and over any word which brings God to mind. Lastly he must try to do only those things that he believes God would want him to do. This too is a part of "remembering the Name of God".

Remembering the Name of God is a duty which must be performed regularly. As a man continues day by day to perform this duty he gradually attains the perfect peace which, for Nanak, is salvation. He does this while continuing to lead an ordinary life, living as a member of a family and working as other men do. The only difference is that as he learns more about God he also learns to live and act in a way acceptable to God. To find salvation one must also show love towards other people.

RELIGIOUS STUDIES DEPT.
KINGSDALE SCHOOL

From the Second Guru to the Fifth

During the years following his travels Nanak gathered around him an increasing number of Sikhs. The word Sikh means "disciple" and this is exactly what his followers were. When the time of his death drew near Nanak decided that he should appoint a successor to follow him as Guru. His sons both expected that the honour should be theirs. Nanak, however, chose one of his disciples. This man, Angad, thus became the second Guru of the Sikhs.

Guru Angad was followed by the third Guru, Amar Das. It was the fourth Guru, Ram Das, who founded the town of Amritsar and made it the principal Sikh centre. Ever since his time this town has been the holiest of all places for Sikhs. It is in Amritsar that their most famous shrine, the Golden Temple, is to be found.

Two important events mark the period of the fifth Guru. The fourth Guru was followed by his son Arjan, and it was Guru Arjan who decided to provide the Sikhs with a holy scripture. The third Guru had already collected the hymns of the first three Gurus. To these Arjan added his own works and those of his father, together with a few more by other religious teachers. These he dictated to a scribe and in this way produced a

21

large volume of sacred hymns. This volume was at first known simply as the Granth Sahib, or "Holy Book". Later, as we shall see, it came to be known as the Guru Granth Sahib.

Guru Arjan's scripture

The second important feature of Guru Arjan's period was the kind of death which he died in 1606. He had earlier been put in prison by the governor of the Punjab and in 1606 he was executed. Up to this time the Gurus and their Sikhs had been left in peace by the rulers of India. Now, however, the number of Sikhs was increasing and the rulers were becoming worried. Their decision to execute Guru Arjan marks the beginning of a long period of trouble and war between the Sikhs of the Punjab and the rulers of India. It was during this period that the Sikhs rose to fame as brave soldiers and in the end it was they who won.

RELIGIOUS STUDIES DEPT.
KINGSDALE SCHOOL

Early Wars

The first battles between the Sikhs and the rulers of India were fought during the time of the sixth Guru. India was governed at this time by a line of emperors called the Mughals. The Mughal emperor ruled the Punjab through a governor who lived in the city of Lahore. It was this governor who first made war on the Sikhs.

The three battles which took place during the time of the sixth Guru, Hargobind, were very small, but they showed the Sikhs that they would have to protect themselves. The seventh Guru did this by moving away from the plains of the Punjab into a hilly place. There he was left in peace. His son, the eighth Guru, died while only a child. It was not until the time of the ninth Guru that troubles began again.

Instead of staying in the hills the ninth Guru used to make journeys into the plains in order to visit his Sikhs. Although he did no harm to anyone he was regarded as a dangerous man by the emperor. Orders were given for him to be seized and put in prison. When he refused to give up his faith he was executed in Delhi by command of the emperor.

A New Brotherhood

After the Guru had been executed some Sikhs managed to carry away his head. They took it back to the hills and laid it before his son, the new Guru. The new Guru, Gobind Singh, realised that a very serious situation faced his Sikhs. Soon there would be an attempt to destroy the Sikh faith altogether.

How could the Sikhs be made strong enough to resist the emperor's attack? The new Guru considered this for a long time, and then sent a command to his Sikhs. As many as could come were to gather before him on an appointed day. This was in the year 1699. The day was to be a very important one for the Sikhs.

Khalsa emblem

When the Sikhs gathered to meet the Guru he was nowhere to be seen. All they found was a tent. More and more Sikhs arrived until a large crowd had assembled before the tent. Suddenly it opened and the Guru stood before them, holding in his hand a naked sword. The crowd fell silent and the Guru spoke. To their horror the crowd heard him demanding the head of one of his Sikhs.

At first no one came forward to offer his head and the Guru had to repeat his demand. At last one brave Sikh went up to the Guru. He was taken into the tent and the crowd heard the sound of the sword falling. When the Guru returned alone they could see that the sword was stained with blood.

The Guru then demanded the head of a second Sikh. After a pause another Sikh offered to give his life. He too was taken into the tent and again the sound of the sword could be heard. Still the Guru was not satisfied.

Only when five Sikhs had been led into the tent did the Guru finally cease to demand more heads. He drew back the front of the tent and to their surprise the crowd saw before them the five Sikhs, all alive and unharmed. Beside them lay five beheaded goats.

The Guru then explained what he had been doing. His plan, he said, was to found a new brotherhood, one which would be strong and brave enough to resist the attacks of those who wished to destroy the Sikhs. The first members of this new brotherhood must be men whose bravery had been tested. The five who had offered their heads had shown that they were truly brave and so they were to be the first members.

The Guru baptised the five with water, after which he himself received baptism from their hands. All men and women who were willing to join the new brotherhood were then invited to come forward and be baptised in the same way.

After the baptism was over the Guru preached a sermon to those who had joined the new brotherhood of Sikhs. Because they were to form a new army they must accept a new way of life. They must promise never to cut their hair and always to wear four articles. These were to be a comb for their hair, a steel bangle, a dagger, and a particular kind of breeches. Smoking was strictly forbidden and a new name was to be added to their old one. All Sikh men were to add the name Singh to their old name, and all women were to add the name Kaur.

The new brotherhood was to be called the Khalsa. All who belonged to it were to be "soldier-saints", men and women who were prepared to fight for the defence of justice and their religion.

A New Kind of Guru

Guru Gobind Singh's brotherhood was soon put to the test. His army was attacked by a Mughal governor and several bitter battles followed. Many Sikhs were killed in these battles, but the Khalsa brotherhood was not destroyed. Although its numbers may have been fewer its spirit grew stronger. In the end the Mughal emperor gave up trying to crush the Sikhs. During his later years Guru Gobind Singh lived in peace.

When Guru Gobind Singh died in 1708 a big change took place. Ever since the time of the fourth Guru each new Guru had been the son of an earlier Guru. Although Guru Gobind Singh had four sons, all had been killed, two by the Mughal governor and two in battle. This meant that there was no one to take his place.

The answer to this problem was not to be some other person, not even a relative of the last Guru. The Sikhs were now to have an entirely different kind of Guru. Before he died Guru Gobind Singh is said to have declared that Sikhs should ever after regard their sacred scripture and their brotherhood as the Guru.

The scripture was the collection of hymns which had been written down at the command of the fifth Guru. Because these hymns contained the teachings of Guru

Guru Granth Sahib

Nanak and other early Gurus they could always be accepted as the voice of the Guru, one which would never die. Previously the scripture had been called the Granth Sahib or "Holy Book". Now it was to be known as the Guru Granth Sahib, "the Holy Book which is Guru".

The voice of the undying Guru was also to be heard in the Khalsa brotherhood. Whenever the Sikhs gathered together in council they were to do so in the presence of the Guru Granth Sahib. Their debates were to be conducted in the spirit of the Gurus' teachings and their decisions were to be accepted by all Sikhs as the decision of the undying ever-present Guru. The scripture and the brotherhood thus spoke as the Guru. Sikhs were to read and follow the holy scripture. They were also to accept the decisions of the Khalsa brotherhood.

A Time of Suffering

The peace with the Mughal rulers was to be only a brief one. Soon after the death of Guru Gobind Singh fighting once again started in the Punjab between the Mughal forces and the Sikhs. This time the Mughals were determined to crush the Sikhs completely and their attempt to do so was to last for many years.

These were years of great suffering for the Sikhs. Many of them left their homes to take refuge in hills and wastelands. There they continued to resist the rulers of the Punjab. Several stories of great heroism have come down from this period.

Victory for the Sikhs

The Mughal rulers had other enemies besides the Sikhs. One of these was the king of Afghanistan. In 1747 this king began a series of invasions, coming down the Khyber Pass to attack the Punjab and northern India. His armies were strong enough to defeat the Mughals, but not strong enough to conquer northern India. A time of great confusion came upon the Punjab.

Sikhs in battle

This confusion favoured the Sikhs. They grouped themselves into twelve warrior bands and now that the old enemy had been destroyed they attacked their new enemy, the invader from Afghanistan. In the end he too was defeated and the Punjab was left to the twelve bands of Sikhs.

Each band had its own leader and these leaders now found that they could not agree amongst themselves. Fighting started once again, this time Sikh against Sikh. In the end one of the twelve leaders overcame the others and became master of the Punjab. This man was named Ranjit Singh. In 1799 he captured the capital city of Lahore and in 1800 took the title of Maharajah, or Emperor of the Punjab.

Maharajah Ranjit Singh

Ranjit Singh was not a handsome man. He was small in size, his skin had been badly marked by small-pox, and he had lost one eye. The small maharajah was, however, a mighty leader and within a few short years he had built a kingdom strong enough to withstand all enemies as long as he was alive. These were the days when British power was growing in India and already the British had brought almost the whole country under their control. Even they were not willing to challenge the Sikh kingdom of Ranjit Singh.

31

Many Europeans visited the court of Ranjit Singh in
Lahore and several wrote reports of what they saw. The
courtiers who surrounded the maharajah were dressed
in jewels and splendid robes. Ranjit Singh himself, however, always appeared in simple white garments,
although sometimes he wore on his arm the famous

Ranjit Singh

diamond called Koh-i-noor. This diamond he had obtained after defeating the rulers of Afghanistan. Later it was captured by the British and can now be seen in the Tower of London as one of the Crown Jewels.

When receiving visitors in court Ranjit Singh often sat in a chair which to some Europeans looked rather like a hip-bath. This chair was also captured by the British after Ranjit Singh's death. It is now in the Victoria and Albert Museum in London.

The forty years of Ranjit Singh's reign were years of Sikh power and greatness. Sikh armies extended the boundaries of the Punjab kingdom to the south, west, and north. Ranjit Singh was a loyal Sikh and generous to religious institutions. New Sikh temples were built and old ones were given grants of land. The dome and upper storey of the main temple in Amritsar were covered with gold leaf and for this reason the building has ever since been known as the Golden Temple.

The Fall of the Punjab Kingdom

Some Europeans were mere visitors to the Punjab. Many more came because they could hope for employment as soldiers. Ranjit Singh hired several Europeans (mainly French) to train his new army and cast his cannon. The strength of this new army was one of the main reasons why the British never attacked him.

Battle against the British

As long as Ranjit Singh was alive his Sikh kingdom remained strong and the British kept outside its borders. When he died in 1839, however, there was no firm ruler to follow him. Once again the Punjab sank into confusion. The army was still powerful, but it lacked competent and loyal leaders to direct it.

Six years after the death of Ranjit Singh war broke out between the Sikh army and the British. Although the Sikhs fought bravely they were soon deserted by their leaders and in the end were forced to surrender. Part of the Punjab was taken by the British in 1846.

A second war began three years later. At first the British were seriously defeated by the Sikhs. They managed to recover, however, and in the end the whole of the Punjab became a part of British India. Duleep Singh, the child emperor, was removed from his throne and later sent to England. There he lived for many years as an English country gentleman in Elveden village in Thetford, Suffolk. His grave and that of his wife may be seen beside the church in the village graveyard.

Duleep Singh

The Sikhs Today

Although the Sikh armies had been defeated their reputation remained and many Sikhs later enlisted as
soldiers in the British Indian Army. Their bravery and
their impressive appearance won them a special place in
the Indian Army and their reputation soon spread to
other parts of the world.

Although Sikhs are particularly well known as
soldiers it would be a mistake to regard this as their
only claim to fame, or to think that all Sikhs are inter-
ested in military employment. Most of the Sikhs who
enlist in the army come from the rural areas of the
Punjab, from its villages rather than from its towns.
Others remain in the villages where they distinguish
themselves as farmers. Much of the Punjab soil is very
fertile and Sikh cultivators use it to produce large crops
of wheat. In many places they are able to grow two or
even three crops each year. Sugar cane is another crop
which is widely grown.

Agriculture is the principal activity of village Sikhs
and military service comes second. Those who live in
towns follow different occupations. Many are shop-
keepers. Others are traders, lawyers, or teachers. All
Sikhs, whether villagers or townspeople, are expected to

Sikh taxi-drivers

earn their living by their own labour. One never sees a Sikh beggar.

Sikhs have also distinguished themselves in two other areas of Indian life. The first is transport. If you hire a taxi in New Delhi or Calcutta you will often find that it is driven by a Sikh. You may also notice on the roads of India that many of the large freight-trucks are in the hands of Sikh drivers.

The other activity in which Sikhs play an important part is sport. This applies particularly to hockey and athletics. International hockey teams from India always have several Sikhs amongst their members. This is true of both men's and women's teams.

The Sikh Duty

There is a popular Sikh saying which runs as follows:
Nam japo, *kirat karo*, *vand chako*.
Repeat the Name, do your work and give to others a portion of what you earn.
A short translation could be:
"Devotion, labour, and charity".

The saying is a popular one because it sums up the duty of a Sikh so well. To understand the first of its three parts we must return to the teachings of Guru Nanak and remind ourselves of the meaning he attached to the word "Name". Anything that concerns God or tells us something about God may be understood as a part of the "Name of God". To "repeat the Name" means remembering God, meditating on Him, and singing His praises.

There are several ways in which the Sikh of today may fulfil his daily duty to "remember the Name". If he is a devout person he will repeat certain parts of the sacred scripture at three set times of the day. When he awakes in the morning he will first bathe and then will recite a poem by Guru Nanak entitled *Japji Sahib*. During the early evening he will sing a short series of hymns, and immediately before sleeping he will sing another brief series.

Singing hymns at these three times is a customary method of "remembering" or "repeating the Name". Needless to say they are not the only times at which a Sikh will sing hymns by the Gurus, nor are the hymns set down for these three occasions the only hymns he ever sings. A Sikh will sing softly to himself at any time of the day and as he does so he will be recalling something about God. He may do this as he walks to work, as he drives his tractor, or when he relaxes at home in the evening. Instead of singing a hymn he may utter a single word or brief phrase which reminds him of God or of the Gurus who gave him his knowledge of God. Whether singing a complete hymn or murmuring a single word he will be "repeating the Name" and so fulfilling one of the chief obligations of a true Sikh.

Sikhs farming

The second obligation is honest labour. For some people religion consists only in worship and some even withdraw from all other activity in order to devote themselves to prayer and meditation. A Sikh would respect the right of others to do this, but he would not accept it as the proper course for himself. For him it is a religious duty to earn his bread by his own labours.

He will, however, recognise that some are unable to work for their living. Some are too old, others may be crippled in some way, and yet others may never receive the opportunity to earn enough to support themselves. This imposes on him his third obligation. From his own earnings he is expected to give a portion for the support of those in genuine need. Charity is the third of his religious duties.

To these three aspects of the Sikh's duty a fourth should be added. A particularly important word for all Sikhs is *seva* or "service". This is understood in two senses. First, there is the duty of service rendered to the Guru. This is performed in such ways as reading the scriptures so that others may hear, making an offering to the upkeep of a temple, or helping with its repairs and daily cleaning. The second sense is service to others. Service to a man is service to God. By helping others a Sikh fulfils a sacred religious duty.

The Holy Book

Reading the Guru Granth Sahib

We have already seen how the fifth Guru produced a sacred volume called the Granth Sahib and how this volume later came to be called the Guru Granth Sahib. For Sikhs the Granth Sahib or "Holy Book" is truly the Guru. Anything written in it must be accepted as the sacred word of the Guru. Honour shown to the Granth Sahib is honour to the Guru.

For this reason the sacred scripture occupies a place of very special importance in the Sikh religion. Every Sikh home is expected to possess a copy and to show unfailing respect towards it. All Sikh ceremonies are conducted in the presence of a copy and important

42

decisions may be made by opening it at random. The passage which appears when the volume is opened in this manner is accepted as the Guru's guidance in the making of the decision. If a copy is being taken from one place to another it should be properly carried on the bearer's head. This is to show honour to the Guru.

The Guru Granth Sahib consists of hymns by the Gurus and by other religious teachers whose works were accepted by the fifth Guru. The only portion which is recited rather than sung is Guru Nanak's *Japji Sahib*, the poem which devout Sikhs repeat each morning. The

Bowing before the Guru Granth Sahib

language is like modern Punjabi, but somewhat more difficult to understand as the contents of the sacred volume were all composed several hundred years ago. The script, which is called Gurmukhi, is the script used for writing Punjabi today.

Devout Sikhs are expected to read a portion of the scripture every day. On special occasions such as a marriage or a funeral an "unbroken reading" will be arranged. A team of readers will take turns at reading so that the entire volume is read aloud without a break. This ceremony takes approximately forty-eight hours. Those who are attending the wedding or funeral are expected to be present when the reading reaches its conclusion. Special prayers are then said on behalf of those for whom the reading has been arranged.

The Gurdwara

Ever since the time of Guru Nanak Sikhs have regularly gathered together to sing the Gurus' hymns. The place where they normally gather for this congregational singing is the temple or gurdwara.

Only one thing is required for a gurdwara and that is a copy of the Guru Granth Sahib. Any building or room in which the sacred scripture is set before the people automatically becomes a gurdwara, graced with the presence of the Guru himself. The principal activity is

Kirtan

still the singing of hymns. This is called *kirtan*. A group of three musicians will normally lead the singing. Others listen to them and from time to time join them in their singing.

When a person enters a gurdwara he will first bow before the Guru Granth Sahib and perhaps make an offering of money. He will then take his seat in the congregation. While *kirtan* is in progress those who are present remain seated, but at certain times all will rise to repeat the prayer called *Ardas*. This is a special prayer which recalls the self-sacrifice of Sikhs in earlier times and the sufferings which they endured for their faith. It also asks God to bestow blessing upon the Sikhs of today.

While a congregation is gathered in a gurdwara there will also be a distribution of *karah prasad*. This is a dish prepared with flour, sugar, and clarified butter.

Gurdwara kitchen

All who are present are expected to take and eat a small portion.

Although hymn-singing is the main activity in a gurdwara religious teaching is not overlooked. Passages from the Gurus' works are explained in much the same way as sermons are preached in churches. There are, however, no priests to do this. In a gurdwara the responsibility must be assumed by the person who is best equipped to carry it out. Sikhs do not have priests.

One particularly interesting feature of the gurdwara is the presence of a kitchen. Close to the room or building housing the Guru Granth Sahib there must always be a place for preparing food and provision for eating it. This serves two purposes. The first is that it provides free food for any who are in need, and the second is that it requires all who gather in the Guru's presence to eat the same food. People who regard others as lower than themselves commonly refuse to eat with those whom they treat as inferior. Sikhs believe that all men are equal. To demonstrate this belief they insist that all who come to the gurdwara should eat together.

Some Famous Gurdwaras

Most gurdwaras are simple buildings, perhaps no more than a single room with a small kitchen attached. Others are splendid structures built of expensive white marble. One of these, the Golden Temple in Amritsar, deserves to be numbered among the world's most famous buildings.

Golden Temple of Amritsar

The larger gurdwaras in India are almost all associated with some important event in the life of one of the ten Gurus. In the case of the Golden Temple the event was the founding of Amritsar by the fourth Guru. A neighbouring gurdwara, Ramsar, commemorates the compiling of the Granth Sahib by his son, the fifth Guru.

As one would expect, the place where the Khalsa brotherhood was founded in 1699 is marked by one of the largest and most impressive of all gurdwaras. It was to the village of Anandpur that Guru Gobind Singh summoned his Sikhs in 1699 and baptised the first members of the Khalsa. The gurdwara which crowns the hill above the village is a particularly important one.

Visitors to Delhi can see another of the major gurdwaras. Situated in the busy street called Chandni Chowk is Gurdwara Sis Ganj. This marks the spot where the ninth Guru was beheaded.

Several important gurdwaras are located in the western portion of the Punjab, now a part of Pakistan. Amongst these are those at Guru Nanak's birthplace (now called Nankana Sahib) and the one which marks the place of the fifth Guru's death in Lahore.

A particularly famous gurdwara is to be found in the village of Hasan Abdal on the road up to the Khyber Pass. This gurdwara bears the name Panja Sahib, or "the Gurdwara of the Holy Palm". According to Sikh tradition Guru Nanak once visited this place, to the

49

Anandpur Sahib

anger and dismay of a holy man who already resided on a hill above the village. To rid himself of the unwelcome visitor the holy man rolled a huge boulder down on Nanak. Seeing it coming the Guru held up his hand and stopped it without difficulty. The imprint of his palm is said to have remained on the rock and for this reason the gurdwara built to mark the spot received the name Panja Sahib.

Most gurdwaras are to be found in India and Pakistan but not all. Wherever Sikhs go they build a gurdwara and there are now many in England, particularly in London and the Midlands. There may be one in your town. If you find one you may be sure of a warm welcome from the local Sikhs. For them it will be pleasant *seva* to show you their gurdwara.

The Sikh Code of Conduct

Ever since the time of the Gurus small books have been issued to show Sikhs what they should believe and how they should behave if they are to be regarded as true Sikhs. The latest of these books has been translated into English and published under the title *Rehat Maryada: A guide to the Sikh Way of Life*. It is from this small book that we can learn about the Sikh code of conduct.

Khalsa symbols

Most features of the Sikh code of conduct go back at least as far as the time of Guru Gobind Singh. Many of them were first introduced when he founded the Khalsa brotherhood in 1699. These include such things as the ban on cutting hair and the prohibition of tobacco.

In the Punjab the ban on cutting hair or shaving beards is still widely observed. It has, however, posed a serious problem for many of the Sikhs who have migrated to England in recent years. In some cases this is because they have been refused employment unless they cut their hair and abandon their turbans. For others it may have been because they dislike doing something which most other people do not do. In the Punjab there are plenty of beards and turbans to be seen. England, however, is a very different place.

Many have attempted to solve the problem by cutting their hair but continuing to call themselves Sikhs. Others who refuse to do this have insisted that the act of cutting their hair deprives them of this right as only the person who leaves his hair untouched can be regarded as a true Sikh. This is an issue which only Sikhs can settle. Others can, however, regard the problem with sympathy. A man should never be refused either work or respect because his religious beliefs forbid him to cut his hair.

Customs and Ceremonies

Four ceremonies are of particular importance to Sikhs. These are the ceremonies associated with the naming of a child, baptism, marriage, and death. All must be conducted in the presence of the Guru Granth Sahib.

When a baby is to be named the family of the child will gather before the Guru Granth Sahib. The volume will be opened at random and the hymn which appears at the top of the left-hand page is sung or intoned. The first letter of the first word of that hymn must be the initial letter of the child's name. The family choose a name beginning with that letter and announce it to all present. If the child is a boy Singh will be added to the chosen name, and if a girl Kaur will be added. Apart from Singh and Kaur there are no names reserved either for boys or girls. For example, a boy may be called Pritam Singh and a girl Pritam Kaur.

Baptism is the next important ceremony, but it is not celebrated until a child has grown to maturity. Five Sikhs, representing the five who offered their lives to Guru Gobind Singh, conduct the actual ceremony while a sixth reads appropriate passages from the scripture. Water and soluble sweets are mixed in a steel bowl by one of the five who for this purpose must use a short

Preparing for baptism

two-edged sword. Prayers are said and each person receiving baptism must drink five times from the sweetened water. Some of the water is sprinkled on the eyes and the hair, and the remainder is then drunk by all who are being baptised. The duties of a Sikh are explained and the newly baptised Sikh must promise always to observe them.

When a marriage is to be performed the bride and groom sit before the Guru Granth Sahib while hymns of praise are sung. They are then asked to stand while prayers are offered and a sermon delivered by the person chosen to conduct the ceremony. (Any Sikh acceptable to both families may perform this service.) Next the bride and groom are asked to bow before the Guru Granth Sahib to show that they both agree to marry. The climax then comes as both walk four times around the Guru Granth Sahib, the bride following the groom and each holding opposite ends of a scarf.

Funerals are conducted in a very simple manner. The body of a deceased Sikh is carried in procession to a place of cremation and is there burnt while appropriate hymns are sung. The nature of the occasion will depend on the age of the deceased person. If a young person has died there will be much grieving by the relatives for a life ended too soon. The death of an old person is, however, a different kind of occasion. Instead of grief there will be thanksgiving and rejoicing for the life of one who lived to a ripe old age. A brass band in a

Punjab street may mean that a wedding is taking place.
It may also herald the funeral procession of someone
who has died after a long and full life.

57

Service, Equality, Tolerance

If an outsider were to list those features of the Sikh religion which particularly impressed him he would almost certainly include some reference to the Sikh ideals of service and equality. The Gurus lived in a society which stressed differences in status rather than equality. In opposition to this the Gurus insisted that all men should be treated as equals and that all in need of help should receive it.

These ideals, taught by the Gurus and passed down by generations of Sikhs, are truly present in the Sikh community of today. The Golden Temple, we are told, has doors on all four sides to show that it is open to all men regardless of their race or creed. Sikhs are a tolerant people, ready to acknowledge the rights of others and to bestow friendship on all who can show the same tolerance. You may already have Sikh friends. If they are true Sikhs they are friends to cherish.

Index

59

INDEX